A Snowy Mountain

A Collection of Life

Poems by
Thomas Hagan

A Snowy Mountain

ISBN: Softcover 978-1-955581-13-4

Copyright © 2021 by Thomas Hagan

All rights reserved. No part of this book may be reproduced or transmitted in any form or by any means, electronic or mechanical, including photocopying, recording, or by any information storage and retrieval system, without permission in writing from the publisher.

Parson's Porch Books is an imprint of Parson's Porch & Company (PP&C) in Cleveland, Tennessee. PP&C is an innovative organization which raises money by publishing books of noted authors, representing all genres. Its face and voice is **David Russell Tullock** (dtullock@parsonsporch.com).

Parson's Porch & Company *turns books into bread & milk* by sharing its profits with the poor.

www.parsonsporch.com

A Snowy Mountain

Contents

Acknowledgements 12
A Snowy Mountain 15
A Peek at Spring 16
A Sweet Spirit 17
A Tree of One 18
An Ode To Tomorrow 19
Camillas on Display 20
Challenges 21
Choices 22
Choose Your Battles' Priorities 23
Computer of the Mind 24
Don't Run 25
Early Morning Light 26
Embrace it Well 27
Giving Today 28
"Guys" 29
Harmony 30
Hello 31
How Do You Know That I Love Thee? 32
I See a Mountain in My View 33
In The By And By 34
Innovation Time Will Set Us Free 35
It is Another Good Day 36
Joy in the Theater 37
Ladder 38
Let the Gold Flow 39

Long Time Ago	40
Looking for a Job	41
Looking for a Starting Place	42
Looking for It	43
Looking for the Who	44
Looking	45
Love, Where Art Thou?	46
Love is on the Vine	47
Magic Carpet Ride	48
Make-Believe	49
March on!	50
Memories of Fall in My Mind	51
Memories Of The Hike	52
My Dance	53
Nature	54
No Goodbyes	55
No Magic Carpet to Ride	56
No Stranger Today	57
Oceans	58
Ode To A Two-Dollar Bill	59
Ode To An RC Cola	60
Ode To Winter	61
Old Friends	62
Passing People	63
Peace	64
People	65
Pew Packing Time	66

Pot of Gold 67
Priorities 68
Purple Is The Color Of The Day 69
Quality Of Life 70
Rain 71
Raindrops 72
Razzle Dazzle 73
Reality Of The Mind 74
Reflections 75
Rejuvenation Time 76
River Flow 77
Rocky Roads Ahead 78
Serenity 79
Shining Star 80
Shout About 81
Shower of Love 82
Someone Else's Dream 83
Spending Time 84
Stars 85
Staying the Course 86
Stop And Go 87
Sweetness On The Vine 88
Taking a Morning Walk 89
Taking The Time 90
The Bind 91
The Collage Of Beauty 92
The Colliery 93

The Dove Is Gone	94
The Face In The Mirror	95
The Gray Zone And This And That	96
The Hiding	97
The Light	98
The Light Is In Me	99
The Line	100
The March And The Man	101
The Mask	102
The Moment	103
The Morning Welcome	104
The Parade	105
The Pathway And The Light	106
The Race	107
The Road To Light	108
The Search For Love	109
The Sounds Of War	110
The Tango On The Sand	111
The Train	112
The Umbrella	113
The Unraveling	114
The Village By The Sea	115
The Waves And The Sand	116
The Winds Of Life	117
Time	118
Today	119
Tomorrow	120

Tomorrow Should Be Today	121
Tranquility	122
Travel The Lands	123
Trilogy	124
Trolley, My Trolley	125
Tumbling	126
Turning Pages	127
Understanding	128
Victory	129
Water	130
Waves	131
What Is Love	132
Wherewithal	133
Who Am I and Maybe I Am You	134
Why Do We Have to Grow Up?	135
Why	136
Without End	137
You Are A Winner	138
Your Past Is Behind You	139

This book is dedicated to my children, Laura, David, Monica, John, and Matthew. They are my proudest accomplishments. I love you, Dad.

Acknowledgements

I would like to thank my daughter, Laura Hagan Sullivan, for providing the photo used on the cover of this book. She is an avid amateur photographer and took the cover photo of this beautiful mountain in Colorado. She provided countless hours helping assemble the poems during the production of this book. Her support and assistance are greatly appreciated. I am also indebted to my friend, Bill Braitsch, who provided technical support during the completion of this book. His assistance cannot be measured in words alone. I would like to also thank my fellow writer, Dr. Paul Saluk. He provided constant encouragement and inspired me to be a better writer in the process. I will forever be grateful to him for his friendship. Lastly, I would like to thank my grandson, Justin Hagan, for his expertise as the copyeditor for my work. He's a bright young man of whom I am very proud.

A Snowy Mountain

Snow is on the mountaintop, and all down the hill
It is time to go downhill skiing, and the ski lift is waiting
The wait-time is short; so get in the chair
Look at the snow-covered area as you move up the hill
It is more than a winter wonderland; it is freedom at last
It's been too long since my skis took me down a hill,
The exhilaration is too much to explain
The experience is like no other, but is many times worth the while
The wind is in your face as you move faster down the slope
All too soon, the trip is at an end, and it is time to begin again
Winter brings back memories and pleasures, which are worth remembering again and again.

A Peek at Spring

A peek at spring as winter continues on with its cold:
The trees are bare of all its leaves and grass is painted a dull brown
Dreams of a warmer weather as spring waits patiently in the wings
The flowers are all asleep and the leaves are waiting for their presence to be known,
The appreciation of spring is hard to ignore;
Spring brings in a newness and a refreshment of the soul
Welcome spring as it fills your garden with flowers everywhere
Open your imagination and paint spring in your mind
Spring will soon be here and greet it as you would an old friend.

A Sweet Spirit

A sweet spirit fills his soul
He is kind and generous
But mostly a sweet spirit fills his soul,
Soft spoken and a tender heart
But mostly a sweet spirit fills his soul,
Time past and distance overcame
But he remains the same
Because a sweet spirit fills his soul,
A reaching out he does fulfill
Always there for others true
And God loves him so
And his sweet spirit will always glow.

A Tree of One

The trees in the forest do not matter
You don't have to count them one-by-one
Because a forest can only be one,
The size and number of the trees are interesting to see
But always remember that the forest may only be one,
If a number was to be, then what would that number be?
It's the shade that is afforded that protects from the sun
The shade of a large tree makes it a forest of only one tree.

An Ode To Tomorrow

Tomorrow is not too far away
But when it arrives it is today,
Today will never be tomorrow
And tomorrow will never be today,
There is no tomorrow as it cannot be
So why do we say tomorrow?
We should wait and say today
I like saying tomorrow as it fades away into today.

Camillas on Display

Camillas on display as spring is on its way
Many buds are waiting to take their turn and burst out
An array of different colors for all to see
Flowers are always a beautiful way of expressing that spring is here,
Birds will soon be singing their songs of praise
Spring is a new awakening that warmth is on the way
The cold days of winter are closing out their stay
Take a walk and view all the beauty on display
Sing a song or two as you stroll along the way
Nature is free for the eyes to enjoy as you rejoice about the new season called spring.

Challenges

Challenges come in many forms, but today is the best way to begin
The world is in turmoil, but you don't have to be dismayed from being you
Move down the road that was meant for you and allow your heart to open wide
You are the best in every way and believe it because it is true
Sweetness and sorrow may come your way, so deal with in your own way
Enjoy today because the challenges are glad that you are there
Smile that beautiful smile that has always been a part of you
Allow the world to understand that you are ready to begin the day
You will meet the day head on and never look back at the sorrows of the past
The world is glad that you are here to make life better, far and near
Challenges will come but you will meet them one-by-one
Welcome to a new day that we all celebrate it as your day.

Choices

Choices are made often throughout the day
Good choices are the best kind to make every day
Often the gray zone surrounds you, but don't be afraid
There is no good or bad but a meeting of the two
Advise may be in order but often it's only up to you,
Don't become hasty but think things through
Often bad choices are hard to undo
Keep a steady hand on you and always think things through,
Each day has challenges of their own, so meet the challenges head on
Many others are on the sideline waiting to assist you if they can
We are all pulling for you in the end.

Choose Your Battles' Priorities

Choose your battles one-by-one
Do not become confused
Choose the battles wisely
And let the battles gently unfold

Few are worth the fight
Overreaction is always in sight
It is the important battles my friend
That we must keep in sight

Ignore most battles
Priorities are the struggle
It is only the few real battles
That will win the fight.

Computer of the Mind

The computer of the mind is such a glorious thing
The images and dreams pass through on their way as they develop you
Creations of the mind can make this world a better place to live,
Don't be afraid to allow the mind to flow in a stream to wherever it wants to go
Freedom of the mind is a gift that should never be placed on hold
Turn the spigot of ideas loose and allow them to take their rightful place.

Don't Run

Don't run from the snow and rain, but embrace it as you would an old friend
Remember the thirst presented by a drought and what a scary thought
The freshness in the air as the moisture pushes away the badness from above,
Appreciate the weather as it comes in many forms even as snow and rain
Allow nature to take its course without the thoughts of grumbling in any form
Come snow and rain as we welcome you to our land and sky,
Let us turn the bother into something good and welcome you over and over again
Come snow and rain and remember you are really our friend.

Early Morning Light

The early morning light brought her into view
I saw her standing there peering across the way
I move beside her, but did not know what to say
She turned your head and brought her face into view,
The excitement had me frozen in stillness never experienced before
My mind was mindless as I tried to gain a composure
The words then began to flow, but only a few
I said hello and then seem to have lost my way
She smiled at me and understood my admiration was for her
An eternity appeared to pass before she began to speak to me,
The voice of an angel flowed from her mouth as she introduced herself
A stroll along the walkway soon ensued and along the way it became hand-in-hand
Joy can occur in so many ways and the early morning light brought joy my way.

Embrace it Well

At one time, love was us and the time was forever
Is forever just a fleeing moment or just a misunderstanding of time?
Love is such a precious gift and so worthy to behold
Holding gentility but always without a letting go,
The rarity of a real love is the beating of the heart
And embracing of the mind and only sweet thoughts,
Love is not a lockbox but always a giving of the soul
Love is renewal each and every day and never to be let go
Embrace it well and be so thankful that it is yours to hold.

Giving Today

The sound of the beautiful voices of birds awakens me;
What a wonderful way to join the day
The clear skies above only added joy to my heart and soul
My body was now rejoicing as to what wonderful opportunities lie ahead
Giving is my only goal today, as gifts to me only take away my opportunity to grow
What can I do today to add to more joy as I travel through the day?
Looking for opportunities as I travel in a most joyful way
With an open heart and mind, it is going to be a beautiful day.

"Guys"

"Guys" are you one or more; because it is hard to understand
"Guys" I see you, but sometimes I only see one
So "guys" means whatever you want it to mean
A word that has many meanings, and not just one
"Guys", are you a girl or a boy
The question is coming again; so please help me understand
Maybe you are a woman or a man
I still do not understand
The meaning is coming, and good feelings are ahead
Now I understand "guys" is singular or plural
And is gender free, and what a wonderful word it has come to be.

Harmony

It is always harmony in my soul as spring starts speaking to me
Today I look out and see greener in the grass
Yesterday the colors were hiding as cold was still in the air
Leaves are appearing on the trees and bushes as far as the eyes can see,
The chirping sounds are once again present for all to hear
The birds are dancing in the air as they fly about
The harmony and love can be felt as winter leaves its cold behind,
A brisk walk is in order as I express a need to join in the celebration
Spring we love you and welcome the beauty that you bring into view.

Hello

Did you say hello or did I say hello first
Does it matter as long as we spoke hello at all?
Greetings with a smile is the way to go;
Let us add some cheer as we march along
A good day is in store so let us open the windows wide
Speak hello to each as they pass by our window today
Maybe our hello will slow them down
It is always time to slow down and enjoy the day
Hello to you and I hope you have a great day.

How Do You Know That I Love Thee?

You need not ask because the knowing is already in the know,
More times than all the stars in the sky
More than all the waves in the sea
More that all the words ever spoken
More than all the miles ever traveled
More than all he dreams ever dreamed
More than all the kisses and hugs ever done
More than ever raindrop that has fallen to soften the earth
My reaching out constantly beckons you to come closer
When we are apart, you will feel that I am still there near you
Don't ever doubt my love because it will be everlasting
There will never be goodbyes, as I am always there by your side;
Reach out and feel my mind, body and soul encompassing you
My everlasting love will always tell you over and over again that I love you
I will always love you more and more with each passing day
My arms are reaching out now across the space of time to hold you in an eternal embrace,
Now and forever more.

I See a Mountain in My View

I see a mountain in my view
I wish you were here to see it too,
There is nothing more beautiful than a mountain view
The flow of a mountain meadow with flowers in view
The walk on the trails brings so much into view
The fragrance of the trees, grass, and all the pretty flowers are always a delight to me
The sunrise and sunset are so heavenly
The ease within the soul brings forth a comfort to me
Come and let us walk together in harmony.

In The By And By

When should I speak, is it time?
Wait your turn in the by and by
Silence is not a way that I can understand
Can I mumble, murmur, or just quake away
Await your time in the by and by
Things are happening and I have things to say
Words can hurt, so stay your stay
People are hurting and I have things to say
Choose your words carefully
Patience, my friend, your time is coming in the by and by.

Innovation Time Will Set Us Free

Innovations will save us yet
Let us forget the debt
Better minds will understand
That innovation is in the wind,
Cures will come, and set us free
Energy here and energy there
Yes, it will be everywhere,
Innovations and technology
I can feel it is on the way
No more need for poverty,
Wars will be a thing unknown
Do not get down, but pull yourself up
Look around because innovation has come to town,
Party labels have no meaning
They were just a stamp that is gone out of date
Toiling has created a generation gap,
It is America's time to innovate
It is time to celebrate
Thirty hours, that is too much
I will work twenty and develop myself
Innovation will place work on the shelf,
It is people time, and dancing in the street
It is go to school time or read a book
It is time to meet the people you have never met
It is sharing time and plenty food to eat
It is the promise we were always supposed to keep
It is relationships, so spend the time
Innovation time is our time.

It is Another Good Day

Enjoy each day because each day is all you may ever have
People have said the future will take care of itself
Meaningless little words which may have no meaning at all
Worrying about the future is not a plan, but just worrying
Take care of today, and live it well my friend
Today has enough variables, and the future variables have yet to be unfurled
Surround yourself with cheerful people, and let the Nay-sayers go their own way
Seek the fresh air of life, and breathe it in with all your might,
It is never too early to smile, and thinking good thoughts is well worth your while
Remember, the only time you failed, is the last time you tried
Remember, also, that picking people up is a blessing you will never forget
Let others see the storm clouds, but for you it is just another blessing to be you.

Joy in the Theater

The joy of the live theater brings about such a glow
Laughter, but sometimes tears are always in reach
The inner emotions have the potential to bubble up
You know you are in good company as the eyes gaze about
The songs, the words come flowing from the front
Pretty soon the mind is in a new world of its own
You settle back and understand that you are in the right place after all
The warmth is present all around, and another feeling is moving about
The overwhelming desire beckons you to return again and again.

Ladder

The ladder has as many rungs as you begin the climb
Climbing for money and greed, but how much is enough?
Is happiness ever on your climb or is that not enough?
Higher and higher, but please be careful and don't fall off
Is the climb going to be gentle or is full steam ahead the goal?
Do you really want to be a star or is another place your desire?
Are you going to be a one-person show or do you need a supporting cast?
There are so many questions to answer before the climb begins.

Let the Gold Flow

Relationships are the gold in the soul
All the people are important, not just a select few
Treat others as your equal and do not look down,
Look across their way and accept them on their level
Do not elevate yourself to a position on high
Humility is a blessing so let it bless you
We are all just people here for a while,
Colors are beautiful so do not close them out
People's inner character is shining so let it come out
Embrace others as you would embrace yourself
Make each day a special day for yourself and others
Let the gold always flow to others as much as to yourself.

Long Time Ago

The forest growth was tall and green
The rivers and streams were clearly seen
The mountain top peaked above the forest green
The air was crisp and clean and the sky was blue
Nature was at ease and comfort with the tenders of the land
The tenders of the land were careful to treat the land as a friend
Then others came along whose ignorance destroyed the land
The forest was destroyed at every turn
The mountaintops were then bare for all to see
The grasslands on the plains were no longer seen
Roads and structures were built everywhere and soon the land was bare.

Looking for a Job

Looking for a job and wonder if there is one around for me
You see, I have been unemployed for far too long,
My body is strong and my mind is bright
It seems that the lines are growing longer with no end in sight
Unemployment is running out and food stamps are tight,
I am getting hungry and do not know what to do
Depression is setting in with no end in sight,
The rich man says self-reliance is in line for me
How can that be when there is no job for me?
The rent man says it is time for me to go
Where am I to go when the money is so slow?
Went to the shelter, but they said it is closed
There are too many people and not enough room
Went to the soup kitchen but the meal was awfully thin
Winter is coming and the cold weather is coming in
Warmth is to be appreciated if I could only find an inn
There is not even a stable that I may lay my poor head
Are there more than a few that need a helping hand?
The lines seem to be long and that cannot be true
Do you believe that maybe a sharing hand will come soon?

Looking for a Starting Place

Looking for a starting place
Why am I here on earth at this time
Am I here to just waste my time?
I appear to myself as too often disagreeing with too much that I see,
Happiness is always created within oneself
If one is in a disarray isn't that hard to do?
It doesn't appear that happiness can be found in a candy store
Where am I to look for a starting place or is that an impossible look
Did my spaceship take me to the wrong place?
There appears to be too much searching and so little to find
I don't want to give up, but searching is so hard to do because I am tired
Maybe tomorrow will be a better day or will it be the same as today
Giving up is not my kind of option
I need to drive on and search for that starting place
Maybe tomorrow will be my lucky day.

Looking for It

Where is "it"
Many keep searching
But it is always in the hiding
What does it look like
Is it drab and gray
Or is it in the shining
Is it loud or is it soft and refining
Can I touch it or can I keep it –
None of that –
Go away consternation
Settle down and keep on with the finding
The "it" is always what you make it.

Looking for the Who

Who took the caring out of the Red White and Blue
Each for their own and the rest need to go
We are crabs in a barrel as we all fall down
Throw the books out the window as learning is for fools,
Brutality is the motto because that's the way to go
Kick them while they are down as mercy has long ago left the store
Throw a kiss of hate and hope that it hits somebody in the face
We use to be united but that was a long time ago
Come closer so I can knock you down is the motto on the doors
The who needs to go so that peace can take its place.

Looking

Looking into the future is a scary thing to do;
The waves of turmoil have me tossing about
Change can be good, but so often it comes with a price
I see the changes in my mind,
Imagination can be a powerful tool
Adjustments will have to be made
I need not run, but I must keep up a steady pace
Challenges will have to be met
We will have to work together or fall on our face,
Adjustments here and adjustments there will have to be made
A calmness must remain with us; because we cannot pull apart
The future can be very good if we only let it
Remove greed from the mix and allow goodness to take its place
Move off the couch and join me and let us work together for good.

Love, Where Art Thou?

Love is more than a song,
Maybe it is a soft caress
Maybe it is the meaningful words of caring
Maybe it is something more
Maybe it is a gentle kiss and the stroking of the hair
Maybe it is flowers on an unexpected day
Maybe it is the sparkle in the eyes
Maybe it is the listening with patient ears
Maybe it is wiping away of the tear
Maybe it is the passion in the heart
Maybe it is the undefinable words of the trust
No matter, it is more than all of that and it is always worth the search.

Love is on the Vine

Love is on the vine
It is waiting for you
Share it with yourself
And then spread the love around,
The time is now and there is no need waiting
I see the glow on your face as you approach the vine
Partake generously, as you will need it for the sharing
Love is priceless but the cost is nothing
You only need to take it from the vine
Do not store it up, there are too many waiting
Hurry on your way and spread the love around
People are smiling as they wait for your gift.

Magic Carpet Ride

Day and night, dreams are magic carpets to ride
Carpets that will embrace you, and wrap you in their arms
Travelling on that carpet can be a beautiful or scary ride
Your imagination may challenge you on that adventure
Creativity of the mind has no borders or time
The ride is up and down, and seemingly without an end
The awakening brings back reality, and a sudden jolt to the mind
Sometimes you struggle to return to the dreams that are now lost in time.

Make-Believe

Why does it have to be
Only in the land of make-believe
Tell me it is not just make-believe,
Can make-believe ever become a reality
That people like each other
And fear is not a part of anyone,
Food is plentiful and it is there for everyone
Shelter is there for you and me
Sunshine and blue skies are a frequency,
Clean water flows in every stream
People do not have to dream of a better day
Because it is already here today.

March on!

See the sunshine when everyone else only sees darkness
Keep your head up when everyone else has theirs down
Walk on the stones, and never fall into the troubled waters of life
Tears may be the lotion of the soul, but laughter can bring great joy to the soul
When the gentle rains fall, do not run, but enjoy a slow movement along your way
Embrace her hand, and give her a smile of encouragement and enjoy the closeness you share
A blanket by the ocean's shores is a place to spend a night and having her by your side
Reactions only brings confusion and an unsettling to the moment
Envelope yourself in a robe of calmness and reaching out
Reaching down is the way; if you are lifting someone else up
Every dream is possible; so it is always too soon to give up on a dream
Applaud the people along the way who encouraged you, and have brightened your path
Today, tomorrow, and every day is a beacon and never a stop-sign
Gather up as many people as you can and have them march with you toward the beacon
Hold their hands, sing a song, or dance if you may, nevertheless, march on!

Memories of Fall in My Mind

The weather is becoming cooler and fall is in the air
Romance seems to be everywhere,
The leaves are turning colors
What a beautiful sight they are,
The strolls are viewed as hand-in-hand
They move closer and closer as they travel along,
The voices are soft and meaningful and are hardly heard;
A kiss is rendered as they stop along the way;
The smiles and freshness on their faces is hard to deny
I see young and old in the visions of my mind
It is like many falls which have come and gone over time.

Memories Of The Hike

A walk down the lane of memories past:
The lane is canopied with fir trees, all so tall
Leaves cover my lane, and provide softness for my feet
Water from the melting snow finds a welcome path in which to flow
The sun makes a valiant attempt to shine through the trees
A spot of warmness is occasionally penetrating on me
The path continues with a steady climb
My legs never tire as it is the beauty of the climb which consumes me
Oh! The awesomeness of the picture at the end
A beautiful lake, and a time to rest my feet
Spreading a blanket on the ground and a time to reflect on the beauty all around
Will I choose an easier route on my return
No matter, because I enjoyed the climb
Will I ever take the time to return
Until that time, my memories must serve me well.

My Dance

The moon is out and provides the light,
The waves crashing against the shore,
Oh the music! The music is always here
The dance floor is hardened sand on the shore;
It stretches North and South in a never ending array of delight
My partner is the wind, and my imagination of those that came before,
The dance tonight is a waltz
Sometimes alone for long periods of time
Now I find a partner once again
Her hair is glistening in the light,
The memories, but I only wish they were real
This is a dedication to a beautiful place which is real
I have been there several times before
The dreams are timeless and often
Daydreams, night dreams, and almost awake dreams
When will I return to have just one more chance to dance?

Nature

Nature's beauty, what a delight
it is all within sight:
The movement of the clouds
The moon shining so bright
The leaves changing colors
The fresh air in a mountain meadow
The snow falling, and each snowflake created with its own design
The rivers flowing over stones so smooth that the waters are orchestrating a symphony of sounds
The fragrance of the trees makes the walk so rewarding that the parade of beauty never ends, but only begins.

No Goodbyes

Love you more than I could ever imagine in a million times
Sweetness gently touches my ears as I hear your voice
The sounds of your caring creates a magical surrounding of love
Come closer and allow me the presence of the wonderment of you
Hold my hand and reassure me that you are really here
It is always too soon for us to be apart
Only together will we travel this great land,
Your caress ensures me that life will always be bright when you are near
There is no me or you but only a uniting of the two
Our love is forever with no interruptions but only growing stronger each day
No goodbyes but always a sweet hello and a steady travel down life's roads.

No Magic Carpet to Ride

Needing and loving do they relate or are they miles apart?
Everyone has a need in their life, but to love is only to love
Bear the need and grasp the beauty of love for love's sake is a stand alone
True love comes in its own right without the attachments of kinds
The wings of life are filled with many grasping of the empty straws
Reach out and be not afraid and let your heart find its way
Holding back can miss the moment as love floats away before your eyes
Risk taking is a scary thing as you throw your heart out to accept the chance for love
There can be no holdbacks and conditions written in stone as love is offered as a bouquet
Giving love a chance is more than words, but an opportunity to open your heart
Taking a chance can be painful and may be a roll of the dice
Rolling the dice is up to you as there is no real advice, but only platitudes from an open heart
When and if love appears, there is no magic carpet to ride because it is all up to you
You alone are in reality all alone when facing the decisions about how to ride the course of love
My heart is with you and I wish you all the best as you pursue the opening of your heart to love.

No Stranger Today

I went out early to see what I could see
Met many people along the way
They were all friendly and kind to me
They all spoke to me, and wished me well for the day
They were all common folks, indeed I must say
No bankers, Wall Streeters, or politicians to see
They were all working people, and very sweet I must say
Many lacked the things that they should have had
But all the money was nowhere to be had
They were the people that create joy and glee
They were not strangers to me.

Oceans

The oceans are rising above the land
The waves are crashing on the shore
The beaches are moving out to sea
The people are moving to wherever they can
"Where to go" is the cry as consternation sits in
There is so much loss and no gain at hand
The blame is being pushed around here and there
The sea does not care about blame as it continues to rise
The homes are no more as they fall into the sea
The cries are growing louder and matches the roars of the sea
Higher ground is the plea and that's where we need to be
The scrambling continues and the sea pays no never mind
The only beauty left is the crashing of the sea.

Ode To A Two-Dollar Bill

I went into a fast-food restaurant and paid with a two-dollar bill
All the employees said, "Sir, that is not real!"
I said it has my President Jefferson on the bill
President Jefferson would not lie to you today, would he
The manager came out and he looked to see
"Sir", he said to me, "that is play money!"
"I cannot put it in the till"
I said that is all the money I have and my hunger is with me still
Now, I do not recommend you use your two-dollar bill
You need to keep it safely under your pillow until it becomes real.

Ode To An RC Cola

What is an RC? Well, I do not know, if I did know
They did not know it because it had been so long ago
The last RC was back in the day
I did believe that the RC was dead
But I saw them on the shelf
Then said to myself
Is this for real?
I thought I was back in the day
Then I awoke and because a real RC was facing me
Yes, can to face, or face to can
No matter, there I saw my old friend, the RC in a can
The can was Royal and with a crown
A beautiful sight, much to my delight.

Ode To Winter

Leaves are falling on the ground
Fall is almost over and winter will soon begin
The frost is in the air and sweater time is near
A burst of energy here and there,
It is cross country skiing time
This has always been dear to me
A trip through the backcountry where few have tread
It is thoughts of snow trails and high altitudes once again,
My eagerness is getting the best of me
Backcountry skiing is more than just great exercise to me
It brings out a relaxation of its own
The eyes move from place to place,
All the sights are beautiful in their own way
Stop wherever you like, because there is no need to hurry
Each season has a beauty of its own
Accept each season as a blessing for you to own.

Old Friends

Where are you my old friends?
Reflections come to me and speak of the good times long past
It seems like time has passed us by, and we are lost in time
Many of you are gone, and many have moved on
How can we meet again when it seems as if you have dropped from the stage of time?
Technology is my friend, but you have hidden yourself well my friends
It is a search, it seems, with no end in sight
Meeting again could bring back that magic of times when we knew each other well
I pray you are doing well, and success has been your mantle in life
Can we relive the past and bring back those joyful moments just one more time?
The search goes on with diligent pursuit knowing that someday and some way our paths will cross
My will is to travel to where you are because it will be well worth the ride
Even if time and space does not allow us to coincide
There are other ways we can meet again, if only in memories cemented in my mind.

Passing People

Passing people on the street always wondering who they are
They are all near and dear to someone, or don't you believe
Never time to stop and learn whether I knew them somewhere in time
It's a hurry up world that keeps spinning around
No time for a chat or a sweet hello
When will the slow-down occur or is the merry-go-round here to stay
I am almost late to work so I better hurry up
Maybe tomorrow will be a slow-down day.

Peace

Peace in the world and peace in ourselves in our time is a wonderful thought
Peace is an illusion for the world but what about us
Peace is like chasing a rubber ball that always keeps moving and is hard to catch
The inner peace is always worth the reward so never give up,
Stress is often surrounding us and the harm comes within us
Does love really capture all or is that an illusion to dismiss
Jobs, traffic jams, and finally being late for work
Never enough time to relax as the road keeps us moving down an uncertain path
Keep the faith that love and peace are real and never give up.

People

People are just people traveling along life's way
No more, no less, but just people one-by-one
People are all different in so many ways,
Different sizes and shapes but all with the embodiment of love
Some round and some thin because they are just people doing the best they can
The moods are up and sometimes down but happiness is awaiting around the bend,
Sometimes happiness and sometimes sadness may appear along the way
Some are darker and some lighter than others but all are beautiful in their own way
They speak many different languages and all are nice to hear
Some are rich and some are poor but people are just people and that should be enough
Their talents are all different as they travel along life's way,
Labeling people is shameful or don't you believe
They all have love stored in their hearts and souls waiting to be released –
People loving people is the goal.

Pew Packing Time

It is pew packing time and revival time
Come on in and hear the testaments
It is the good news you have been waiting for
Hear the songs of joy, and glorify God
Purify your hearts, and sing the praises
Feel the spirit lift you to a higher place,
Get closer because it is pew-packing time
Revival time is all the time, but tonight is special
It is the revived unification of the believer time
Come on in and pack the pews
It is fine to be late, but do come in
It is pew packing time.

Pot of Gold

Where are you in your life today?
Analyzing is something we often do
But the answers are often hiding
But do you really want to know?
Sometimes it's not worth the while to discover
The best pathway is often only one day at a time
Looking back can be painful and regretful to know
Throw the roses of the day high in the air and catch them one by one
Let us make tomorrow better for you and everyone you know
You are shining with the brilliance of gold
Everything about you is precious and we all know it's true
This day is going to be your day with a joy abounding all around you
You are loved, but to make that happen, you must love yourself with a full embrace
March on, beautiful one, because you are the pot of gold waiting for everyone to discover.

Priorities

Priorities is the name of the game
Pull to the left and pull to the right
The failing keeps occurring and no one understands
It's always about priorities my friend,
Special interests and favors for powers that be
It's always been that way so why the interest today?
Change will occur but priorities will be left out of the game.

Purple Is The Color Of The Day

Purple showers coat my garden
And the earth becomes a ray of beauty to fill the day
My purple colors are held aloft by long stem for display
My life ends with the frost
But I reign from spring to frost
Warmth seizes my spirit and I become all aglow each day
My flowers only last for one day
Do not fear because I will be there the next day
Butterflies fill my home and they are always a welcome guest
Purple is my color and such beauty it is
Purple showers are my gift and make for a beautiful day.

Quality Of Life

Quality of life, how nice to hear the sound
It all depends on you as to how the quality plays out
It is not about the money tree or the car in the garage,
Standard of living, find another stage, you do not play here
My walk in the woods or hike along the trails
Has such sweet moments and a joy to my soul,
Talking with others about the joys of life
It cost nothing but it brings such delight
Time with friends, relatives and others
Can bring smiles and laughter, and wipe away the sorrows
Quality of life is on your ball field, so field it well.

Rain

It is raining outside
And the flowers continue to say hello
They welcome the eye with a glow
Freshness in the air that awakens the soul
Can you see the water
It is beginning to flow
The dryness in the ground
Is drinking you know and
The wetness on my brow
Displays this heavenly show.

Raindrops

Gentle drops fall from above
You can once again smell the freshness in the air
The raindrops become larger as the rain continues to fall
The dust and the pollens fall on the ground
The breathing is easy as the air is once again clear
The overcast is of no bother as it shields us from the sun
There is no dreariness here because this is paradise
I walk in the rain with pure delight filling me
I love the rain and I hope you do too.

Razzle Dazzle

I went down to my old haunt, the Razzle Dazzle, just yesterday to see what I could see
I looked and looked to see if my eyes might find a friend of old, but none was there for me
The place had seen better days, but the memories were flashing through my mind as if it were today
The Razzle Dazzle was still there, but it was not the same
The crowd was different, and seemed all so somber
It was if the people did not know why they were there,
The joy days of old were just noises in my head
The laughter and greeting by my friends of times gone was no more
It made me think today that it never happened that way
I only waited a minute or two, and my sadness could not allow me to stay a minute more
Maybe I should never have gone; because the razzle dazzle was no more.

Reality Of The Mind

A reasonable pursuit of reality is a difficult find
Reality is too often hidden in the shadows of the mind
Maybe things are not what they should be
Reality can bring on sadness and a surrounding of fear
Why face reality when you can find a hiding place in the shadows of your mind?
The mind cries out with a warning that reality is on the move
It is time to place reality in the shadows of the mind
Bad things are happening, but let us put them on hold
Tomorrow is another day, and maybe the sun will shine.

Reflections

Looking forward and never looking back
That is the way to travel and you know that
Auto travel is not an easy way
But looking forward is the only way
The views are everywhere to the left and right
But looking forward will make you have a pleasant day
It is the same way in life because every day is a new start
Let the old things pass away because they will just get in your way
Yes, it hard to forget the past but it is the only way to start a new day,
There is always more sunshine than overcast
Do not dwell on the overcast, but look for the sunshine
Sunshine will brighten almost any day
We all have our ups and downs
But downs are just a reflecting place
Count the blessings because they are there
We all have our downs but that gives time for others to help pull us up
Yes, a lot of the pull has to come from within us
But do not deny help from others because their meaning is well
Relationships are the reasons we are here
Yes, there seems to be too many distraction pulling us here and there
Take time for yourself and others that are dear.

Rejuvenation Time

It is a world of incredible people
Most are good and sitting on the high side of life
Sometimes even good people fall on the sidelines
They rest a spell because it is rejuvenation time
Do not get down on people, because they are only people
Sitting on the sideline waiting to be helped up
So they can be on the high side of life
Walking and talking about the sidelines of life
Reach down and pick them up because
Rejuvenation is hand reaching time
Brother to brother and sister to sister
Rejuvenation time should not last forever.

River Flow

Rivers have personalities that do not equate
Rivers run fast as the snow melts or the rains falls
A lazy river appears as the summer sun shines on the water
The river meanders and each turn has an expression of its own,
The whitewater appears as if out of nowhere
The rushing waters are always challenging
But I will wait for the lazy river to send me on my way
Let the river make its own way
Enjoy the scenes which come your way
The same river is never the same,
Each day or season takes on a life of its own
The canoe challenges the waters as we move downstream
Quietness is all about except for the river's flow
The rustling leaves sing their own song
It is as if I had never been here before
The river keeps changing with every flow
The river flows and the beauty only grows
This solitude can never be explained.

Rocky Roads Ahead

Rocky roads are ahead!
Bumping up and down and not knowing where to turn
Look to the left and look to the right
Does it seem that everything is being done?
Can words save us from the undone?
Are we going over the cliff into the abyss?
How far do we have to fall?
Will it hurt that much, or can I live on?
Will tomorrow bring more sorrow and tears to my eyes?
Or, will my star really be that bright?

Serenity

Sweet serenity, you are finally here
Kisses are flowing everywhere
Embraces are so many; it is hard to count
The softness of the caresses are what it is all about,
The walks in the summer rain are a joy to behold
The sounds of guns are nowhere to be found
Health is winning the battle and disease is a thing of the past,
People are finally more important than money
Greed has finally been stamped out
People helping people without a reward
The magnets of industry and finance are giving money so that all can benefit
My people are everybody's people
Because we are finally one in God's house.

Shining Star

When did it all begin to go wrong?
An easy question to answer or don't you believe
When people invaded the earth but that was a long time ago
People come in all forms, as the good and the bad took their place
Some stayed the same and others juggled to find their way
There was no perfection here but the struggles continued on,
There is never a crossroad but only curves in the road
There is no untouched line but too often more holes and rough spots in the road
No road-perfect maps available, so often you are on your own,
Be the best that you can be and try to be better each day
You are a shining star and allowing other to follow your pathway
Lead us on and help keep us out of the pitfalls along the way.

Shout About

Is everything wrong and so little right
Are we in a circle of consternation with no end in sight?
Are we so blinded by everyday matters that the curtain is down
Is everyone for themselves, and will never more be any reaching out?

Should we care anymore, or just be desensitized to the things about
Is the sky really falling, and all we can do is hide beneath the doom which is all about?
Why are we here or should we care?
Lift yourself up and look around
There are so many wonderful people everywhere to be found,
Most people and things are really beautiful if you push away all the bad
Stand on the platform and shout about and push away the curtain of doubt
Shout out that most people are good and they are all around us.

Shower of Love

Love can flow or ebb like so many a stream
What brings it forward into the light of day?
What sustains love like an ever-flowing fountain
Is it the soft caresses and gentle kisses each day?
Why does it cease and go away?
Can love return and begin another day?
Is it the turmoil of the day which turns us away?
Where art thou love which once showered itself on thee?
Return, sweet love, and return to me
It is not the need, but the want of love, which stays the day.

Someone Else's Dream

The faces of desperation are painted with fear
They are black, white, yellow and red
It does not matter the color because the pain is always the same
The causes have for centuries remained the same
The ugliness of greed tightens the noose and strangles the hopes
The hunger is real, and care is always a promise which is never fulfilled
Fear and anger strikes out for all to see, and the greedy say, "how can that be?"
The greed mongers are all tucked away in secure places for none to see
They sit in their places built by greed and feel no guilt
Because caring needs to be someone else's dream.

Spending Time

Spending time along the beach,
The shoes are off and the feet are wet
Strolling slowly hand-and-hand as the waves come in
Smiling and kissing along the way
There is no hurry today,
It is getting late and the moon will soon be out
Moonlight and ocean breezes brings great delight
Spreading a blanket on the sand
Getting closer and saying the words that need to be said,
Planning the future in an imagination of what could be or should be
The waves present the sound and fill the air with music that is tenders to the heart
Does daybreak need ever to come?
Delay is alright with me.

Stars

All the stars in the sky are shining on you because
You are greater than you think you are
You are like a beautiful flower waiting to be unfurled
It is time to show the world that you are special in so many different ways
Say hello to tomorrow because it will be a glorious day; rain and overcast or not
No matter, because you are you and that is what really matters.

Staying the Course

Staying the course can be mighty hard to do
This is especially difficult when you are lost
The fine line is always in play in the staying on course
Pull to the wrong, pull to the right, or staying in place
Confusion is always on the plate,
Waking up early is never enough
The drive through the day is just too long
The guides are still asleep so you're on, you're on
Drive carefully as the course is so long
Persevere my friend and you will win.

Stop And Go

Are the waters still flowing and enough for us to drink?
Are the waters pure as from a high mountain stream?
Do the rivers and lakes have a welcome sign that there is no contamination here?
Can you still see the sky or is pollution blinding the view?
Are gangs still ruling the streets and your freedom has disappeared?
Are drugs and alcohol still ruining lives?
Are the poor still getting poorer and the rich getting richer?
Is hatred playing its ways across the land with glee?
Are nations still in discord and beating the drums of war?
Is there any future worth the while for the young ones or is loss all we can see?
Does turmoil breed more turmoil with no end in sight?
Is there a band without a leader everywhere we look?
Do we have to stop or can we really go?

Sweetness On The Vine

Sweetness on the vine is in the hearts of the people
Respect can bring it out so do not shut it out
A smile here and a smile there can bring on many more smiles
Embracing life with a hug will only bring more hugs
A softer voice here and there will only touch the ears with joy,
Tone it down and see the different responses
Relationships here and relationships there can bring you an ocean of love
Then sweetness on the vine is yours, all yours.

Taking a Morning Walk

Taking a morning walk is always a lovely thing to do
Every day the walk presents a new array of beauty before the eyes
The flora is never the same as newness along the way becomes alive
Maybe it is a new blossom or a jumping frog coming before your eyes
Nature is all free to see and the walk becomes more beautiful every step of the way,
It is always too soon to turn back as the walk proceeds along a gentle path
The blessings are embracing your soul as you move step-by-step along the way
Tomorrow, another walk is waiting for all to see the wonders of nature along the way.

Taking The Time

Life goes on, but I remember the past
The past is where wonderful people have crossed my path
Many people were so much a part of my life
They pushed away the harm that was in my way
They made my life a better place in which to be
Where are they now, that I have the time to search them out
There are thanks and praises I wish to send their way
So many are gone, and I have waited too long,
It seems that tomorrow will be the day
However, the tomorrows past, and I went along my way
Why did I wait so long, and allow triviality to block the day
Yes, I know the phrase do today because tomorrow may never come
I heard it repeatedly over and over in my head
However, it seems that I always dismissed it as if it had never been there
The sorrows reaped upon me by not taking the time to travel their way;
Oh, the words I wanted to tell them are rattling through my mind,
It is the thanks and praises which I never said
My only words are in reprise: Why? Why? Why?
I am so sorry that I never took the time.

The Bind

They say opposites attract
But how can that be
There is nothing there to bind you to me
You go your way, and I go mine
Where is the love that binds?
If I can see what you cannot see
Then what appreciation can there be
If we are so far apart; then maybe the attraction
Should be called an interest from afar
We each have our likes, and that is perfectly alright
There is no doubt that some interests will be far apart
But it is the important commonalities that will create the bind
What are the commonalities that are a must for the bind?
Two lovers must engage, and each discover their own commonalities to secure the bind
Love will follow as the commonalities flow into the bind
Yes, love will be like a meandering river, and stones will cause a few bumps in the flow
But never give up, because love can create such a beautiful song.

The Collage Of Beauty

Love is a collage of beauty within your inner soul
Sometimes it hides away in fear of what it might display
Often the beauty on display is only what we see
It is the beauty beneath the facade which is the mystery of the day
It is the mask again, and we need to understand
The beauty inside may need to wait for another day
Waiting can be well worth the time to fathom the unfolding,
Patience can be a welcoming friend and that can be a precious gift indeed
True beauty is the plurality of many things
A soft voice in the time of distress
Caressing arms which show concern
Words of tenderness which envelope all that is near,
A plurality which is never ending, but coddled with a smile
Deep from inside the reality of beauty comes bursting out
It presents a shower of freshness in the air
Do not suppress another's love which is meant to come out
Embrace it with the encouragement and shouts of joy.

The Colliery

A colliery where day is always night
Where the air is stale and the dust is always in flight
Danger is lurking but preventions are few
The hours are always long and there is little time to think
People grow old long before their time
The lungs are filled with the dreadful black dust
Is there no way out, and why must this go on?
Each day may be the last but the money must come in
They have no other jobs to be filled
So it is down to the colliery and pray this day is not the last.

The Dove Is Gone

The dove came to my garden, but just for a short stay
The dove was small and only beginning to feel the freedom of being on its own
The dove appeared one morning, and my concern was maybe only the ground was its refuge
Was it possible that flight was not possible today, or was it the nourishment of my garden that beckoned my little dove?
There was grass to eat and seeds seemed to be more than enough to store up strength for another day
The beautiful garden had a shower of leaves to provide a coolness, and a shelter from the heat
A stream of water in the little pond was refreshing wetness for its beak
A day later, much to my delight, as a storm was approaching she took flight for the comfort of a tree
My thought was that my dove was gone, but each day she reappeared in my garden in the early morning hours for another day's stay
Yesterday, she flew away in the evening hour, and my sadness was mixed with happiness; as the dove had gone, but maybe the dove had found the way
Maybe, just maybe, the strength was now there after days in the garden, and now the time for flight was right
I go out every morning to view my garden to view the beauty of the plants and flowers in bloom
The reality is that my little dove may never be in my garden again, but maybe another bird may find its way for a short stay.

The Face In The Mirror

The face in the mirror is no longer there
The vanity is empty and sadness is in the air
The times that were, the times are no longer here
Memories are the only treasures and I must keep them dear,
Reunions are always in mind
Did it really happen or only in my mind
Where did it go wrong or was it meant to be
I must hold on for the dreams to come my way
Is it wrong to want things to be the way they used to be
Should I go on and pretend it was a dream that was never to be.

The Gray Zone And This And That

It is left or right and sometimes them or us
The truth remains in the gray zone
It is a little of this and a little of that
Sometimes it is neither this nor that
The questions and answers to this or that
Can become elusive and hide well under this or that
The gray zone can become a frightening place to be
People have to then become willing to think about this or that
It then becomes a movement in the mind, and a stretch at this or that
Sometimes thinking harder is the road to the answer of this or that
Does that mean a compromise or just a new way of thinking about this or that
Sometimes the answer is in view, but can be elusive to you
Give the mind a chance to be used in searching for the answers to this or that.

The Hiding

Where is the strength that once was inside me
Many battles have I seen and of no consequence to my life
Why am I facing defeat without an enemy in sight?
Weakness has never been my companion, as battle-ready has always been my friend
My loneliness should be of no accord because I have many beside me
Into a shell I climb, only to be hiding from myself
There is light in the tunnel no matter how dim it may be
Always enough light to rescue me and allow me to continue on my way.

The Light

There is confusion and dilution everywhere
People are crying and falling into despair
There is an abundance of fear in the air
There is no evidence of hope anywhere
Struggling is an everyday affair
A few have everything and there is little left to share
Is there an answer on the board or will we remain deeper in the grave of life?
They are as small beacons shining ever so bright, but who will bring the light?

The Light Is In Me

Why am I clothed in sorrow
Is it fear that there will be no tomorrow?
Maybe tomorrow will be there
But it may be more of the same sorrow;
Is there no light, but only darkness in the tunnel of life?
Is hope only an indefinable shadow?
Does it have to be that way?
My candle is growing dimmer
It is almost going out;
Will truth bring back the light?
I am reaching out, and my strength is strong
How far do I have to reach to find the light?
Has the light always been there
But has my own darkness snuffed it out?
Has the light always been in me?
Yes and all I have to do is let it out!

The Line

Good morning! Good morning!
America, are you still there?
I cannot seem to find you in all this racial strife
People hating people is something I cannot understand
War is evermore on the horizon, and soon we may all be dead
Preacher-men tell us whom to hate, so that we may join in
Starve the people and throw them away
Are people important anyway?
Where did my country go?
I am looking hard, you know
There is a protest over there, but should I join them?
Is there any meaning or answers to be found?
Barriers and prisons abound
Drums! Drums! They are loud, but not very clear
Lock them up and take away the jobs
Because they do not need money anyway
I would like to take a stand, but where does the line begin?

The March And The Man

A ride up the road, and the trip was not very far
Getting off the bus it was visible that the ground was covered with snow
The man could be heard taking his oath, and then talking some more
This young Marine was soon assembled for the beginning of the march
It seems as though there was only one street free of the white fluffy stuff
In the middle of the street, the trolley track was still frozen and very slippery indeed
The march proceeded with packs on our backs
A step there and again and again we marched along
Finally, a turn to the right for a short while, then it was left again, and finally to an abrupt stop
From the outside column and looking straight across, the speaking man and his lady were not far away
His tasseled hair and smile was always there
First, a look at the man then the lady came into view
The lady was as beautiful in person as I knew she would be
Then one final glance at the man and the march began again
It seems like yesterday that I was there face-to-face with the man but it was so long ago

However, something as beautiful as that can never leave your mind.

The Mask

Everyone is wearing the mask
There is no shame to bear
There is no one-size-fits-all,
Some are thicker than they need to be
Others are far too thin, and open for too many to see
Hiding is not a game, but protection you see
Protection from the mask is alright, my friends
Privacy can be a virtue so do not amend
Unveil carefully because destruction is always at hand
You need to know you, but remember the mask is your friend.

The Moment

The moment is a precious thing
Appreciate and savor the joys it can bring
Wrap it in the cloth of happiness and sail on
The moment is so fleeting, but it can return
The times may be dire, and the moment of happiness returns
A saving grace by the moment of time
Hold it for only a second, and freshness reappears
Life is all about relationships and the capture of moments of time.

The Morning Welcome

A welcome each morning as I look out
They are always smiling and dressed to the hilt
My eyes are wide open, and sleep is no more
Their hello is like a soft shout sounding in my ear
What a welcomed sight to begin each day
Good morning, they say, and it is going to be a glorious day
The radiance of their colors is a blessing indeed
The walk is never the same as my feet travel about
Looking here and looking there with head in a spin
How fortunate to be able to see my garden again.

The Parade

Failure is a word which turns me pale,
It has no place in our lexicon
This word should hide itself out of view
Many people cower at the whisper of this word
Come out wherever you are, and face the brightness of the day
This is your day because it was made for you to shine
And shine you will, and blossom into the person you were meant to be
The only time a setback faces you is the last time you try
Setbacks are temporary, and are never meant to stay
Come and join the parade because we are willing to march with you
March with you, we will, until the end of the parade.

The Pathway And The Light

Many have lost their way
They cannot see the pathway, as the pathway is dark and hidden away
The time will come and a move will be made to show the light of day,
There will be times in your life when the pathway is hidden
Open your heart and fall on your knees
Pray to God to show you the light;
The pathway will lead you home
The pathway is never far away
You just need the light to show you the way.

The Race

The race cannot begin nor should it ever
Don't enter the race, but just keep up a steady pace
Let us walk together and talk about the good things that are meant to be
Let us stop along the trail and eat the blackberries on the vines
Nature's scenes are such a treat as we view the flowers and the fruits along the way
Let us enjoy life together as it's meant to be in all its glory
Forget the flaws because they are of no matter and will only slow us down
The path appears to be made of gold because that is all we appear to see
Can this walk not last forever in its peace and tranquility?
Life should be what you want it to be, so don't let circumstances always get in the way.

The Road To Light

I was traveling down the road
With no particular place to go
I saw a ray of sunshine
However, the sun was not out
The light was covering me all about
The brightest was showing me the way
As I began to understand
What the road was all about
Sometimes the road ends
With nothing in sight
Travel on and let it lead you
To the place you need to go
Do not be afraid to travel on
Because you are on the road to light.

The Search For Love

Is love around the corner, or only far away?
Can it be dreamed up or is it real
Is love whimsical and a fantasy of the heart
Is love a wish which will never come true
Why all these questions about something we all hold so dear
More questions than answers is not what I want to hear
I need a pathway which will lead me to love
Is love really kind, gentle, patient, and jealousy free
Is it unselfish giving in such a timeless way
Is love covered with a blanket of goodness and trust
Will the search be long
Maybe the search should start in my own heart.

The Sounds Of War

Boom! Boom! Boom! These are the sounds of war
The tanks are rolling once again
The ships are bobbing up and down on the sea as if they were toys in a bathtub
Cannons and missiles point here and there
No direction in particular as to where they should be
It is a peace mission you see, because it is the way it has to be
The people are wailing loudly, "Give peace a chance"
The leaders shout back, "It is time for war!"

Children dying on the fields of battle with nowhere to hide
It does not matter what the leaders say, because it is the cost of war you see;
Boom! Boom! Boom! The war goes on, as it is making money for someone, you see
Lives are here today and gone tomorrow with little concern because the war must go on!

Boom! Boom! Boom! These are the sounds of war
The cemeteries tell the stories of wars in the past, and reverence is paid, but it does not last
The wars go on as they have in the past, and they must last and last
Boom! Boom! Boom! This is the sound of war.

The Tango On The Sand

It is time to dance on the solid sands once again
The ocean is heard with its constant song from the waves
The cliffs are seen on the other side as a reminder of times past
The wind is gently blowing and placing a coolness on my face
There is no partner this time or shall I wait?
Maybe she will return and dance with me one more time
It has been too long since my feet have reached this beautiful spot
Is she really returning, but how long must I wait?
The energy for the dance is welling up in my feet
Shall it be the tango, a waltz, or something new?
The tango has always been my favorite dance
Is that her in the red dress which is flowing in the wind
Is it my imagination or whimsical aspirations or is it for real?
She seems to be so far away, and my eyes are straining to see
It is as if my heart was youthful again, and can be heard from afar
She seems to be moving faster as she sees me with my arms waving her on
Surely, we can dance for several hours before the tide comes in
The tango it is, and we begin to dance once again on the ocean sands.

The Train

Is the world spinning out of control
Is everything wrong and nothing right
We are on a fast moving train with no time to stop
More issues than answers and that is a lock
Confusion, delusions, and terrifying times
Lives are being lived here and there and nowhere
The pathway seems to move to the left and right
Is there an in-between or another way we can go?
Party labels, the leaders say, is the way to go
However, should they not only represent you and me.

The Umbrella

An umbrella opened wide over me today as morning broke
The umbrella shut out all hated that surrounded me
My mind was cleared of all the fears that have ever embodied me
I could now see all the good things that had surrounded me
It was like I was being awakened from a dark sleep,
I saw no evil as it was being shut out and not allowed to come in
It was much like I was washed clean and was born again
I am now able to see the good that had been hiding behind the bad
It is a beautiful day where there is more love than hate as I go about my day
My umbrella is such a wonderful gift that will now always be a part of me
The realization is that it was always up to me to accept the umbrella and not push it away.

The Unraveling

Love is up and love is down
But love is always around
Compassion, sweetness, and a never-ending parade
A mystery of unraveling the inner sanctums of light
The light that is unknown to all but the beauty of love
The journey is long but well worth the wait
Unraveling takes time but how sweet is the taste of love
Reaching out and reaching in but what delight
Unravel my precious love because it is always worth the wait.

The Village By The Sea

There was a time not so long ago I lived in a village by the sea
It was as quaint as any village could ever be
The village by the sea, and it was filled with calm, hush, and tranquility
Every evening time was spent looking westward at sunset from the docks by the sea
The sunset was never the same, but magical as it could be
I loved that little village by the sea, because it was more than home to me
It was a place to rest the heart and soul at the end of each day; by the docks, you see
Someday soon, there will be time for me to return to that little dock and see the
sunset again as if for the first time.

The Waves And The Sand

The tides come in and the tides go out;
The waves play a beautiful song on the shore
Sometimes there is loudness in the roar
Others times the waves have a more gentle song to play
The lull of the waves have a mesmerizing way to capture the soul
Stay the night, for there is no reason to abandon the sand
The cool breeze and ocean spray will provide more reasons to stay
The blanket on the sand with a beautiful lady in hand
Oh the memories of that night will never leave my mind.

The Winds Of Life

When did the winds begin to blow?
Did they howl or gently push you on to tomorrow?
Did you win the game of life or struggle on the plains?
Did you curse the day you were born or cheer and embrace victory along the way?
Is every day a great day no matter the course it takes?
Do you love your enemies or do you have none?
Do you praise every day as a new beginning or just dwell on the past?
Even howling winds can bring back the fresh air of life if you only let it!!

Time

There is movement and then it is gone
Fleeting images are all we see
Why do we call it time
When it is always gone
It seems it never waits for me
Time is so fast and it is always gone past
Slow down and let me rest.

Today

Tomorrow seems so far away
There is plenty time to delay
My eye is only on today
There are still so many things to do
Live well my friends, and concentrate on today
Soon enough tomorrow will be today
Do things well again as you did yesterday
Do not look for praise, but just do the best you can
Pretend that no one is looking and look straight ahead
Appreciate each day and smile as much as you can
Have a great day because you know you can.

Tomorrow

Tomorrow is not just another day, but an opportunity
An opportunity to be better than you were the day before
New refreshing thoughts will push away the evils of the day
Another opportunity to lift people up and not down
Lift them as high as you can, or, if need be, place them on your shoulders
Respect people even if you do not understand them
People are not throwaways, but some need a little brushing off
Life is not a straight line, and the rules are not always laid out
Meandering happens now and then, but the rainbow is just ahead
Steady my friend, remember that opportunities lie just ahead.

Tomorrow Should Be Today

Tomorrow is not that far away
Let us not make it just another day
Yes, jump for joy all the way
Smiling and saying hello as you travel along the day
Lifting people up and never pushing them down
Always contributing and never holding back
But understanding that it is relationships that count
Tomorrow should be today.

Tranquility

Vibrations of tranquility have overcome me today
My concerns are so far away and freedom is my new friend
Walking in the lanes of beauty everywhere as I travel down the pathways of life
Everyone is smiling my way and no frowns can be found anywhere
It is a glorious day with everyone working together
There are tears, but only the tears of joy can be seen
Helpfulness is the song of the day
No one is turning away, but only staying to make this a very special day
The bands are playing soft tunes which are fragrances of love
Why cannot everyday resemble the joy of this day.

Travel The Lands

Why the travel, my friend?
Have you not seen all you want to see?
Yes, there are still many beautiful sights to see
The question is how many must you see
It is not a must, my friend, but a desire within
There are more languages to be learned and cultures to understand
New people are wonderful to meet
Learn to accept the differences as best you can
Look for the positives as one travels the lands
The boat is waiting so say good-bye to your friends.

Trilogy

The trilogy of love branches out and forms the bouquet of love
The trilogy showers out a ray of sunshine truly covered with everything good
The love of caring stands by with arms reaching out
The love of silence remains until words of praise come pouring out
A love of listening to those that are speaking and with a desire to hear them out,
The trilogy is just the beginning and with no end in sight
There is always the bending down to lift someone up
The trilogy provides a foundation to build a better life
Allow the trilogy of love to guide you as you move through life.

Trolley, My Trolley

Trolleys, my trolleys, where did you go, I surely miss you
Did you fall off the tracks, and buried yourself in the history books?
Will my search take me to scrap yards, where you must reign supreme?
You were such a nostalgic icon of the beautiful days of the past
The ride on those tracks was a peaceful memory that I cannot forget
Your brothers and sisters still remain on the tracks down in New Orleans
My travels took me there only last year, and my ride was a sweetness beyond compare,
The powers that be removed you from those tracks and there was nothing I could do.
You were a good one, you really were; no pollution, and only an electric cable to spur you on
The push was for buses with their pollution in tow, and they sent you away, and sorrow filled the day
It was greed, you know, that sent you on your way, but I want you to know I think of you often
I heard a rumor the other day that some places are thinking of bringing you back
You have rested too long, and I will be there when you get back
I will ride you often and tell you how much pleasure you shower on all of us
My feet are holding me steady at the trolley stop awaiting your return.

Tumbling

Is tumbling always down, why not up?
How many blocks have to tumble down before we are not up?
When does the tumbling begin and when does it end?
How long has it been since the tumbling began?
Do we have to tumble to the end?
Does tumbling have a return or is it always the abyss?

Turning Pages

Turning pages is what life is about, or maybe it is more than that
Sometimes it must be alright to stay a while longer before the page is turned
There will always be gains and losses along the way
Are the easy paths the way to go, or should we not try the bumpy roads
Bumps can jar the spirit and send one into vistas yet unknown
Rocky roads can create new songs which need to be sung
The tall grasses of life you do not need to be afeard
Hold your compass steady, and proceed at your own pace
Hold on to your own beliefs, but do not fear learning new ideas
Knowledge can be a frightening awakening, but evaluate its worth
Look for the good and you will find it sometimes hidden, but most often in plain sight.

Understanding

Understanding can be most difficult to do
This is especially hard to do when the world is piling up more bearers for you
The truths and the lies appear to blend into one pile of nonsense
Life often needs a hiding place and a clearing of the mind,
What use to be right is now apparently wrong
The words are changing meanings and it is becoming difficult to communicate
Is there a place for me in a world that is attempting to confuse me
My chart of many goals is constantly changing and it is hard to walk a straight line
Why am I here is often the question I hear in my ear
Life is always worth living, but I am pleading for directions today
My tunnel of light needs to be brightened up
I am beginning to see a rainbow as I reach for more directions today
Tomorrow will be a brighter day because I always have faith to lead me.

Victory

The victory is not always in winning
Often a person can gain more by losing
Come to think of it, I do not know what winning is
Is it a score, a grade, or going through the door?
Do not let others define victory
They do not know the meaning of victory for you
You determine victory because you are the minder
Yes, you are the minder of the score.

Water

Rainy days mean a lot to me
The water doesn't bother me, as I float away
My thoughts are with the many places that are water free
Drought is not a pretty thing, and brings a lot of heartache it's way
Water is such a precious thing, and it rejuvenates the earth wherever it falls
Water storage is always on my mind because there has to be a better way
There is no substitute for water no matter how we try
Waterfalls here, but not always there
Concern is a good thing, because water should be on your mind
Solving the water challenges will soon be on the way; because there is no other way.

Waves

How many waves are in the sea
Are they always there night and day
Does the moon really spoon them on their way?
Waves are crashing on my shore
Their marriage is in the sands that they sweep away
Waves to ride forevermore
Large waves and small waves touching shore
The sounds are lulling, and I only want to hear them more.

What Is Love

Love is more than pretty words or guidelines which to pursue
It is an inner feeling and has no design
It is magical and all-consuming to each other
It is a reaching out without expectations of a return
Our bible of love is within ourselves
Love should not be complicated but should represent the softer side within
It is a sharing of ideas and dreams of the way things should be
Let us walk along the ocean shores
Let the waves sound their beautiful song and melt our hearts together as we embrace.

Wherewithal

Do you have the wherewithal, you may ask;
Stopping before the end may be a pleasant way to go
Motivation can drive you on to your goals
Knowledge for knowledge's sake is not a bad inventory to accumulate
Keeping the mind open to new ideas will drive you on
Don't ever count yourself out because setbacks can occur
Believe in yourself and others will believe in you too
Grab the brass ring because it's yours to keep
I see the goal line and you will see it soon
Success is yours to keep and it's worth the try.

Who Am I and Maybe I Am You

Who am I? Maybe I am you,
"I am beauty on display" is just another lie told by you and me
I am the person that you will never know
I am beauty and ugliness wrapped into one
I am dressed nice and sometimes dressed in rags as well
I am the creature in the dungeon
I am the light that shines above
I am the devil and the angel that lives above and below
I am the flyer and the crawler as I move across the earth
I am the people that continue to ruin the earth
Scars and destruction are too often my goals
Finally, I am the people that may destroy their very souls.

Why Do We Have to Grow Up?

The why is always in the mix
Why do we have to grow up?
Even children may have a tinge of bad
Good is really in their makeup,
Adulthood can too often to be a bad place to reside
The ups and downs of life appear to overwhelm them
They soon fall down and never seem to get up
A helping hand would be nice to have
Others say their hands are full
When will we learn that everyone has a breaking point
Is helping others not a way to help yourself?

Why

Why don't people get along better than they do?
Are nationally, cultures, race and religion the stumbling blocks lying in the way?
Are not all people alike in more ways than not?
What is the gain in being angry or hating when love places a glow in the heart?
Is it greed, jealousy, or just plain stupidity that grinds the wheels of love to a stop?
Happiness comes from within so in reality it not up to everyone to get right with themselves
When people love themselves then the love for others will have a starting place
Someday the dreams of a world of peace and love may take their rightful place.

Without End

The wind is softly touching her hair
The moonlight is all a glee as it shines on her face
My eyes meet hers and my feet are frozen in place
Now I see beauty as never seen before
I gently take her hand
And smile a smile, as never before
She smiles back, and my lips caress her in a loving embrace
We then continue to walk along the lake
The pace is slow, and always stopping ever so frequently for another embrace
Never questioning, "Will this time ever end?"
Is this only a dream?
Dreams can be beautiful, but they always end
Dreams end all too quickly
I want this softness, to go on for another day
Yes, go on forever without an end.

You Are A Winner

Look up and never down
The stars always look brighter
When you believe in yourself
Better is never good enough
The climb has only just begun
Improve every day a little at a time
Time can be in your favor
However, do not dottle too long
March along, but always keep up the pace
The finish line is always only about today
Long-term goals are nice, but the prize is today
Never dwell on the slow days
Because tomorrow will be glorious
Everyone is in your corner and pulling for you
Sometimes it is hard to see them
They seem to be hiding, but they are still there
Smile a smile that glows
Because you are a winner, after all.

Your Past Is Behind You

You never really know what the next day has in store
Hopefully, it will be filled with only goodness and kindness
You deserve the best, and nothing less, and no sadness
May your days be filled with floods of joy that bring happiness
Don't turn back to the past, because that is behind you
Greet others with smiles and they will reciprocate with smiles of their own
Be respectful and respect will surround you
You deserve the best and I pray it will fulfill you.

www.ingramcontent.com/pod-product-compliance
Lightning Source LLC
Chambersburg PA
CBHW070614010526
44118CB00012B/1514